Wolfgang Amadeus
Mozart
The Life, Times, & Music Series

Wolfgang Amadeus Mozart

The Life, Times, & Music Series

Julie Koerner

Friedman/Fairfax Publishers

A FRIEDMAN/FAIRFAX BOOK

ISBN 0-9627134-9-X

THE LIFE, TIMES, & MUSIC SERIES:
WOLFGANG AMADEUS MOZART
was prepared and produced by
Friedman/Fairfax Publishers
15 West 26th Street
New York, New York 10010

Editor: Nathaniel Marunas
Art Director: Jeff Batzli
Photography Editor: Grace How
Production Director: Karen Matsu Greenberg

Printed in the United States of America

Contents

Introduction 8

Family 10

Early Travels 14

First Published Works 19

The Prodigy 20

Poor Health 23

La finta semplice—Mozart's First Opera 27

In Italy 28

A New Archbishop in Salzburg 33

Aloisia Weber 35

Anna Maria Dies 37

Return to Salzburg 39

Marriage to Constanze 41

Domestic Life 42

Le Nozze di Figaro 50

Eine Kleine Nachtmusik 51

Leopold's Death 52

Don Giovanni 53

Symphony No. 40 in G Minor

     and the Late Works 58

Requiem in D Minor 64

Additional Listening 68

For Further Reading 69

Index 70

Introduction

olfgang Amadeus Mozart was one of the most gifted musicians—and certainly one of the most prolific—to have ever lived. But in Salzburg in 1756, the year of his birth, the prevailing attitude toward musicians was quite a bit different than it is today—or perhaps indifferent would be a better word.

Austria then was part of the Holy Roman Empire, a loose confederation of principalities and royal houses in central Europe, nominally ruled by the Habsburg emperor, Francis I.

Salzburg, Austria, during its cultural enlightenment.

Salzburg was deemed important enough in A.D. *798 to become the seat for an archbishopric. Nearly five hundred years later, in 1278, the Salzburg archbishops were recognized as princes of the Holy Roman Empire, commencing the rule of the first in a succession of prince-archbishops who, together with wealthy burghers and traders, transformed Salzburg into a city of significant cultural and political influence.*

In 1756, the year of Mozart's birth, the prince-archbishop of Salzburg was Count Sigismund von Schrattenbach. The highest position

a musician could attain in his court orchestra was that of orchestra director, or Kappellmeister. The appointment paid a modest salary; in exchange for money and local prestige, the Kappellmeister was expected to compose music on demand for court occasions, religious Masses, and various state and social functions. But court-appointed musicians might also be expected to perform valet duties, thus lowering their status to little more than that of servant.

Family

Wolfgang was born to Leopold and Anna Maria Pertl Mozart. Anna Maria bore seven children, only two of whom survived infancy: Maria Anna, nicknamed Nannerl, born in 1751, and Johannes Chrysostomus Wolfgangus Theophilus (later Wolfgang Amadeus), born on January 27, 1756.

Salzburg flat where Wolfgang Amadeus Mozart was born on January 27, 1756.

Photograph of a portrait of Mozart at four years old.

The Mozarts' home was a musical one. Leopold was assistant *Kappellmeister* and played violin in Archbishop Sigismund's orchestra. He composed religious music for the court, trained the choir, and was able to supplement his income by teaching violin. He also wrote what is thought to be the first comprehensive written instruction for students of the violin, *Search for a Basic Violin Method*, published the year Wolfgang was born. It is of interest not only for its musicological content, which is still studied today, but as a historical record of the music world in the eighteenth century.

About Leopold's influence on Wolfgang, two things are clear: Leopold, who did have the benefit of education, instilled in his son a devout Catholicism that would stay with him throughout his life; and Leopold was the family decision-maker. During Mozart's childhood, the father was manager, social director, and agent. While he loved his entire family, it is apparent that he invested all of his interest and energy in promoting and exploiting Wolfgang's talents.

Both Mozart children showed superior musical ability at an early age. There are many stories about how Wolfgang first displayed his genius: he was said, at age three, to have imitated everything Leopold taught Nannerl during her violin lessons; at four, Mozart repeated precisely several parts of an orchestral piece

Leopold, a violinist in the archbishop's orchestra, taught both his children to play the violin.

The Eighteenth-Century Musical Pantheon

The most influential musician in the eighteenth century was Johann Sebastian Bach, whose death in 1750 brought to an end the Baroque era of music. His thousands of compositions, many of them breathtakingly intricate and crafted with mathematical precision, arguably qualify him as the greatest composer of all time.

Bach's youngest son, Johann Christian Bach, was also a gifted musician who composed church music, operas, sonatas for the piano and harpsichord, and chamber and orchestral music. J. C. Bach had a direct influence on Mozart, who visited him in England.

George Frederick Handel, like J. S. Bach a legend of the High Baroque, was also a German-born musician who lived in England and is remembered best for his operas and brilliant choral music.

Franz Joseph Haydn, an Austrian, was prolific through the second half of the century, and is now highly regarded for his keyboard sonatas and variations, oratorios,

Handwritten manuscript of a composition by Franz Joseph Haydn.

church music, piano trios, operas, string quartets, and more than one hundred symphonies.

Johann Michael Haydn, Franz Joseph's younger brother, lived in Salzburg and was the prince-archbishop's *Kappellmeister* in 1762. The Haydn brothers would both come to hold Wolfgang Amadeus Mozart's music in high regard. The younger Haydn, a respected composer in his own right, was a longtime friend of Mozart and had some influence on the latter's music.

Franz Joseph Haydn.

Johann Sebastian Bach.

George Frederick Handel.

Portrait of Leopold Mozart in 1762, at age forty-two.

after hearing them only twice; and no one disputes that Mozart composed original music by the age of five. By all accounts, Wolfgang Mozart was a prodigy whose musical ability was unprecedented.

One can only imagine Leopold's wonder and awe as his two children amused themselves and others with virtuoso performances practically before they could walk. As a professional musician, he appreciated the potential value of their talents and resolved to share those talents with the world. It was a decision that would lead to a childhood of travel throughout Europe for Wolfgang and his sister.

Early Travels

The first venture undertaken by the Mozart family was a short trip to Munich in early 1762 to perform for Elector of Bavaria Maximilian Joseph III. Both Mozart children were received so enthusiastically

that Leopold requested a leave of absence from his orchestra post in Salzburg and moved his family to imperial Vienna, where he hoped to find an even larger audience for his talented offspring.

Portrait of Mozart as a young boy, painted by Pietro Antonio Lorenzoni.

The city fulfilled all of Leopold's ambitious dreams for his children. They per- formed in the homes of chan- cellors, dukes, ambassadors, princes and princesses, and finally, in the court of Empress Maria Thérèse, who had become coregent of the Holy Roman Empire with her son, Joseph II, following the death of her husband, Emperor Francis I. Wolfgang even became a young

On his first trip to Vienna, the prodigy performed at court.

The seven-year-old Mozart plays violin for the Austrian court.

friend of the Archduchess Marie Antoinette, Maria Thérèse's daughter, who later became Queen of France (and later still lost her head during the French Revolution).

At the age of six, Wolfgang had no knowledge of protocol concerning royalty or aristocracy. One of Leopold's letters tells how Wolfgang, upon meeting the Empress Maria Thérèse, jumped on her lap and embraced her. The child was affable, outgoing, and charming. After several months of travel, the family returned to Salzburg, laden with jewels, clothes, and other gifts presented to the Mozart children.

Wolfgang and Nannerl perform for Empress Maria Thérèse.

Mozart is introduced to Madame Pompadour.

The success of the Vienna journey encouraged Leopold to prepare for an even more extensive tour that would include the more distant cities of Paris and London. Again, Leopold requested leave from his Salzburg post. Along the way, his children performed in Munich, Augsburg, and Brussels. Leopold arranged private and public concerts, accepting gifts and collecting concert fees whenever possible. In January of 1764, the Mozarts performed in Paris before King Louis XV.

Map of Mozart's three major tours, originating from Salzburg and Vienna.

The frontispiece to the sonatas dedicated to Queen Victoria.

A page from the manuscript of the Andante for Piano, K. 9b, written by Mozart at age seven.

First Published Works

In Paris that same year, Wolfgang had his music (in this case, several keyboard sonatas) published for the first time. Sonatas were a popular form at the time because "amateur" musicians, mostly the moneyed and the aristocracy, could play them. Mozart's sonatas contained optional violin accompaniment. These sonatas were published as Opus 1 and Opus 2, and later cataloged as K. 6–7 and K. 8–9 in the Köchel cataloging system.

The Köchel Catalog

Ludwig Ritter von Köchel was an Austrian lawyer and a successful mineralogist who also happened to be a devoted Mozart fan. In 1851, he began to make a list of Mozart's works, in the order in which they were written. His project culminated eleven years later with the publication of the most comprehensive catalog of any composer's works. The catalog included the date and place of publication, and other details about each piece. Köchel organized Mozart's works by assigning each one a K. (for Köchel) number that corresponded to the work's position in the overall chronology. Although the catalog has been revised several times as music scholars have discovered more recent or more accurate information, especially about chronology, Mozart's works are still referred to by their Köchel catalog numbers.

Dr. Ludwig Ritter von Köchel, whose system of cataloging Mozart's works is still in use.

The Prodigy

Until the end of 1766, the Mozarts continued to travel through England, Holland, and back through France and Germany. Stories spread throughout Europe of the prodigy; sometimes Wolfgang was even called a "magician." His performances may have sometimes resembled an act, for at times he was required to play with a white cloth covering his hands. Once, an audience claimed that a finger ring was enabling Wolfgang to play the music, so he was instructed to remove it. Of course, he could play just as well without it. Another time he was put in a room by himself and told to write some music—to prove that he was really the composer.

Formal portrait of Great Britain's King George III, for whom Wolfgang and Nannerl performed in 1764.

In London, the children played for King George III. And it was also in London, in the spring of 1764, that Leopold fell seriously ill, forcing the family to refrain from traveling for several weeks. During this period, Mozart composed his first symphonies. Both the No. 1 in E-flat,

Mozart's spinet, now in the Mozart Museum in Salzburg.

Johann Christian Bach, youngest son of Johann Sebastian Bach, befriended young Mozart in London.

K. 16, and the No. 4 in D Major, K. 19, show the heavy influence of his newfound friend, Johann Christian Bach, the youngest son of the great Baroque composer Johann Sebastian Bach.

During all of their travels, Wolfgang and his sister, Nannerl, performed together. But while Nannerl showed great talent as a musician, Wolfgang's genius became more and more apparent. In The Hague during the summer of 1765, Nannerl contracted intestinal typhoid, and Wolfgang performed his first solo concert. Leopold understood that Wolfgang was the prodigy, and soon began to focus his attention on his only son.

Poor Health

It is questionable whether Leopold showed the best judgment in insisting that Wolfgang continually travel throughout his childhood. As a result of this constant touring, his childhood was spent performing and living "on the road," a circumstance that seriously compromised his already weak constitution.

Thus, it is impossible to evaluate Mozart's life without discussing the many illnesses that affected him, both directly and indirectly. There is no question that Mozart was a sickly child who suffered doubly from the vague diagnoses and questionable treatments administered by doctors of his day. By most accounts, when Mozart wasn't traveling, he was ill. (Medical science at the time was relatively primitive; remember, of Leopold and Anna Maria's seven children, only Wolfgang and Nannerl survived infancy.)

Mozart family, 1781. The portrait is by Johann Nepomuk della Croce. Note portrait of Anna Maria in the background.

During Mozart's first trip to Vienna in 1762, he became ill with what doctors then thought was scarlet fever (it may have been an unrelated skin ailment called erythema nodosum). During his childhood, Wolfgang was twice stricken with rheumatic fever. At The

Portrait of Wolfgang at around age ten.

Hague, as soon as Nannerl recovered from typhoid fever, Wolfgang contracted the disease. Mozart also suffered from smallpox and, throughout his adolescence, from several other diseases, all of which contributed to his death at the young age of thirty-five.

View of the Thames River in London, where the Mozarts first visited in 1764.

Formal portrait of Nannerl Mozart dressed for a court performance.

The Mozarts were in Vienna during the smallpox epidemic of 1767. Their landlord and many of their neighbors were stricken. Leopold tried desperately to find other accommodations for his family to protect them from exposure to the ghastly disease. As it turned out, he moved only himself and his son to nearby Bohemia, leaving behind his wife and daughter. Young Wolfgang contracted smallpox anyway, but recovered.

La finta semplice –
Mozart's First Opera

It was during this period in Vienna that Leopold, in his capacity as his son's "theatrical agent," decided that young Mozart should compose a piece for the theater. It took a bit of hustling, but Wolfgang was finally commissioned to write the opera *La finta semplice* (The Make-Believe Simpleton), K. 51. Out of jealousy, local composers protested that it was impossible for a twelve-year-old to compose so quickly and so well. Some critics even went so far as to accuse Leopold of being the true composer. Despite Leopold and Wolfgang's efforts, their critics managed to delay the premiere of *La finta semplice*, which wasn't performed until the following year in Salzburg.

Prince-Archbishop Sigismund had decided to show his faith in Mozart. It was at the Archbishop's request that *La finta semplice* was produced; the Archbishop even designated a special theater for the performance. Wolfgang was also named *Konzertmeister*, a non-paying job, but one of considerable prestige and distinction at court. In addition, Sigismund gave Leopold some money and his permission to take Wolfgang to Italy.

The Role of the Copyist

The copyist was important to composers, who often hand-copied their own original manuscripts, which were themselves handwritten. Not trusting the competence or the motives of others, Leopold often served as the copyist for Wolfgang's works, or Mozart would copy them himself. Royal courts employed copyists who could be hired free-lance, and the Mozarts sometimes used their services. Mozart relied upon three major copyists, never fully trusting any of them. It was not unusual for dishonest copyists to change a composer's work, pass it off as their own, or sell it to someone else who would then broker or exploit the music without the composer's knowledge or permission.

In Italy

Italy at the time was a mecca of musical experimentation and innovation. Florence, Venice, Milan, Verona, Naples, Mantua, and Rome were especially alive with music and opera. Leopold and his son made three trips from Salzburg to Italy between 1769 and 1770.

Wolfgang was adored by the Italians. Likewise, he adored the music, the people, and their attitudes toward music and toward him. He played before counts, dukes, the archduke, and the pope,

A view of the Stairs of the Giants in Venice.

Wolfgang is admitted to the Academia Filarmonica and given diplomas in Bologna and Rome.

who awarded Mozart the Order of the Golden Spur. He was presented diplomas from the Academia Filarmonica in Rome and Bologna. He performed concerts and conducted orchestras. Mozart composed the opera *Mitridate, rè di Ponto*, K. 87, on his first trip to Italy. He later composed the operas *Lucio Silla*, K. 135, and *Ascanio in Alba*, K. 111. In addition, young Wolfgang wrote concerti, masses, and serenatas.

Rome's Piazza del Popolo in 1770.

A view of the Arno River and several bridges in Florence.

During this period of travel back and forth between Salzburg and Italy, Mozart made a significant detour to Munich for the production of another of his operas, *La finta giardiniera* (The Make-Believe Gardener), K. 196.

Program from Mozart's opera Mitridate, rè di Ponto *first performed in Milan in 1770.*

Italian Opera

Opera had its initial outburst of growth and popularity in Italy, where it fell into two categories: serious and comic. *Opera seria* (serious) was originally written for, and often loosely about, the aristocracy. Its mythological or historical stories featured kings, generals, and royalty, and tended to present a noble portrait of loyalty and honor without much conflict. The actors who played the roles in opera seria tended to be aristocrats themselves, who, as was fashionable in that day, had had extensive vocal training. The music written for them tended to be complex, with long and difficult passages.

Opera buffa (comic, though Mozart said it meant "crazy") was less serious, and often drew characterizations based on human failings. Its characters were from the middle or lower classes. Musical parts in opera buffa were more varied than in opera seria, probably because its performers were less skilled. By the middle of the century, characters from the lower aristocracy started to appear in opera buffa, opening story lines to a much broader spectrum, including interaction between the classes. Opera buffa frequently included a finale sung by all or most of the cast.

The character Bazile from the Italian comic opera Almaviva (later known as The Barber of Seville)*. Taken from a story by Pierre Beaumarchais that was written before* The Marriage of Figaro, *Rossini's opera opened in Milan after Mozart's success with* Figaro.

A New Archbishop in Salzburg

The Mozarts returned to Salzburg in December 1771, just one day before the death of Prince-Archbishop Sigismund. In the new year, Sigismund was succeeded by the nobleman Count Hieronymous von Colloredo-Waldersee, who launched a campaign to align church music closer to the spirit of the Enlightenment.

An anonymous Austrian portrait of Mozart after his stay in Prague in 1787.

Prince-Archbishop Hieronymous von Colloredo-Waldersee, whose succession did not benefit Mozart's career.

Hieronymous retained both Leopold and Wolfgang in the employ of the court, but relations were never very good between him and the Mozarts, who continued to ask to be excused from duty to pursue Wolfgang's career. Hieronymous treated his *Konzertmeister* with little respect, even seating him with servants at meals. Finally, perhaps because the Mozarts petitioned for leave once too often, Hieronymous dismissed them both.

One goal of the Mozarts' travels was to find steady work and income. Archduke Ferdinand wanted to commission young Wolfgang, but the archduke's mother, Empress Marie Thérèse, objected to keeping "unnecessary" people on the payroll. Following their dismissal from the Salzburg court, there was no reliable income at all. It was decided that Wolfgang would continue his travels with his mother as chaperon, while Leopold and Nannerl remained in Salzburg, earning money by teaching music.

Wolfgang's sister, Maria Anna, was nicknamed Nannerl.

Aloisia Weber

Mozart and his mother made many stops en route to Paris. In Mannheim, he met two women who would become significant in his life: his cousin Maria Anna Thekla, called "Bäsle," with whom he formed an immediate friendship, and Aloisia Weber, an excellent singer with whom Wolfgang fell in love. Because of Aloisia, Wolfgang and his mother remained in Mannheim for several months. Leopold, frustrated in Salzburg, urged them in his letters to continue on to Paris.

Mozart met singer Aloisia Weber in Mannheim and fell in love.

Maria Anna Thekla, called Bäsle by her cousin Wolfgang, became a close friend of Mozart.

Now in his twenties, Wolfgang was no longer a prodigy, and the public fascination with him had clearly waned. He and his mother finally reached Paris, where Mozart performed several of his new compositions, but received no commissions for new work.

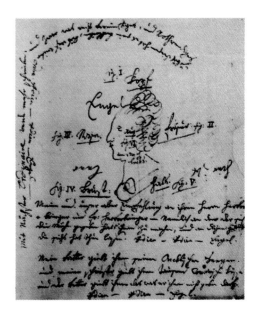

Part of a letter from Mozart to Bäsle dated May 10, 1779.

Anna Maria Dies

Suddenly, unexpectedly, Wolfgang's mother fell ill with fever in Paris and died. Initially obeying her wishes, Wolfgang did not call a doctor when she first became ill. But as her condition worsened, a doctor was finally summoned. He diagnosed "internal inflammation," which, like other diagnoses of that time, tells us little today, and could have characterized any number of ailments.

Wolfgang's mother, Anna Maria, in a detail from a family portrait.

Paris as it looked near the time of Anna Maria's death.

Immediately after his mother's death, Wolfgang wrote two letters. The first was to his father and sister, telling them Anna Maria was gravely ill. He wanted to prepare them for the worst. Then he wrote a longtime Salzburg friend, Jesuit priest Joseph Bullinger, and asked that he tell Leopold and Nannerl the tragic news about Anna Maria. Soon after, in a letter to his father and sister, Mozart begged their forgiveness for his lack of courage and candor, explaining he had only hoped to soften the shock.

Early title page from Mozart's Sonata for Violin in A Major, K. 293b (1778).

Return to Salzburg

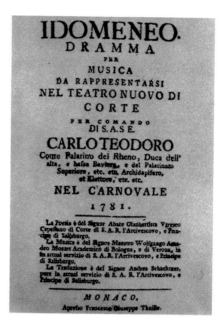

Title page from Mozart's opera Idomeneo, *commissioned in 1779.*

As Leopold was pressuring Wolfgang to stop wasting his time in Paris and come home to earn some money, and as several openings had developed in the Salzburg orchestra, Mozart did return to Salzburg, where his fortunes improved considerably, if only temporarily. The ever-vigilant Leopold was able to secure an appointment for his son as court organist as well as *Konzertmeister*. For this, Mozart was given a

The Collegiate Church in Salzburg, where Mozart's Missa Brevis in D Minor (1769), K. 61a, was first performed.

generous salary, plus the promise of freedom to travel and to produce other music. But court politics and his already uneasy relationship with the archbishop soon conspired against this run of good luck.

In 1779, Mozart received a commission from Munich to compose an opera called *Idomeneo*, K. 366. The opera was a great success, but during its run, Archbishop Hieronymous, in what may have been simply a gratuitous exercise of power, commanded Mozart to join him in Vienna. In another incident, the archbishop ordered Mozart to entertain him with a concert, knowing that by doing so, he would prevent Wolfgang from attending a concert at which Emperor Joseph II, a potential patron, would be present.

Mozart returned to Aloisia Weber only to learn she had married Josef Lange, an actor.

It soon became clear to Mozart that he didn't really have the freedom he had been promised. In 1781 he asked the archbishop to be relieved of his duties. The archbishop literally had him kicked out the door. Unemployed again, Mozart turned to the Weber family, now in Vienna, to find solace with Aloisia, his love of four years earlier. But Aloisia had married an actor. Undaunted, Mozart developed a strong attachment to Aloisia's younger sister Constanze, and resolved to stay in Vienna to be near her.

Constanze Weber Mozart.

Marriage to Constanze

Among other projects he undertook during that time, Mozart helped organize a subscription concert series and worked on the opera *Die Entführung aus dem Serail* (The Abduction from the Seraglio), K. 384, the production of which, for a variety of reasons, was delayed for a year. *Die Entführung* came to be known as a "fiancée's opera" because it encompassed the same period of time as Wolfgang's courtship of Constanze. This courtship was scrutinized by both families. Constanze's mother practically refused to let her out of the house until Wolfgang committed to writing his intention to marry. (Constanze tore up the agreement.) Leopold strongly opposed a marriage before his son was able to earn a steady income. Perhaps Leopold also worried that Wolfgang might concentrate less on his music. Despite all these objections, Constanze and Wolfgang were married in August 1782.

Domestic Life

Throughout the 1780s, Mozart lived in Vienna. He taught many pupils, performed concerts, composed new pieces, and had his works published, many for the first time, by the Viennese music publisher Artaria. Wolfgang and Constanze had a busy, social life in which she shared his interest in both music and good times. By all accounts the two were supportive partners.

Their first child, Leopold, was born in June of 1783. He died two months later. During the nine years of their marriage, Constanze bore Mozart six children, only two of whom survived infancy.

This portrait of Mozart by Josef Lange was Constanze's favorite rendering of the great musician.

An Evening's Entertainment

On Christmas Eve, 1781, Mozart was summoned to the Emperor's court to perform for Joseph II and the Russian Grand Duchess Maria Feodorovna. What was unusual about this command performance was that another popular composer and performer, Muzio Clementi, had also been invited. This was to be a competition between the two for the entertainment of the Emperor and his guest. Together and separately, Mozart and Clementi played piano, read unfamiliar music, and improvised music of their own. They were then required to critique each other in writing. It is said that Joseph, who had a wager on Mozart, won his bet by all accounts, including those of Clementi and Mozart.

Muzio Clementi, with whom Mozart had a musical duel.

Patronage and the Musical Arts

Because it was virtually impossible to earn a substantial (or sometimes even subsistence-level) income as a salaried member of the chamber or court, musicians in the eighteenth century relied on patrons for commissions. Since Mozart had performed so often for the pleasure of others, he had several friends who helped him make acquaintances and receive commissions. Baron Gottfried Bernhard van Swieten was Mozart's patron and close friend from the time the twelve-year-old composer rehearsed his first opera, *La finta semplice* (in van Swieten's home), until Wolfgang's death in 1791. Count Johann Joseph Anton Thun-Hohenstein and his family frequently hosted Mozart in several cities; Mozart in turn dedicated Symphony No. 36 in C Major (the "Linz" Symphony), K. 425, to the Count in 1783. Count Karl Joseph Firmian made many introductions on Mozart's behalf in Italy, and helped him get the commission for the opera *Mitridate, rè di Ponto*. And Mozart's famous Serenade in D Major for Orchestra (the "Haffner" Serenade), K. 250, was commissioned by his friend Siegmund Haffner on the occasion of the wedding of his sister Marie Elisabeth in 1776.

A Hans Hansen portrait (1798) of Wolfgang and Constanze's two living children, Franz Xavier, born 1791, and Karl Thomas, born 1784.

Soon after baby Leopold's death, Mozart performed the major part of the Mass in C Minor, K. 417a, which he never completed. Constanze, a singer like her sister, sang one of the soprano parts. Mozart and Constanze lived well during the early part of their marriage. Mozart was able to earn a steady income. He was a master pianist (he was also a virtuoso violinist) and received healthy payments for his performances in public concerts and before royalty. In 1785, at the height of his popularity as a performer, Mozart composed and performed the Piano Concerto No. 21 in C, K. 467, now called "Elvira Madigan." This concerto, brim-

Spinet played by Mozart

ming with quiet elegance and lush beauty, is an example of Mozart's most spirited and enlightened compositions.

As a child, Wolfgang had been outgoing and precocious; as an adult he was much the same. He stood five feet four inches; he was frail and pale, most likely the result of his childhood illnesses and strenuous travels. He loved to fraternize, play billiards, play practical jokes, and laugh. His letters show him to have been bawdy, even vulgar; but bawdiness was the style among his family and peers. He was clearly opinionated and vocal, and no doubt he offended many of the people whose work he did not respect. Not one to conform, Mozart powdered his light reddish hair and wore no wig as an adult, a change in custom that was becoming popular with the "younger generation."

Vienna's Mehlgrube Concert Hall, where Mozart first played his Piano Concerto in D Minor, K. 466, in 1785.

Portrait of Joseph Haydn, who became an admirer and friend of Mozart.

Both Mozarts loved to dress in high fashion, and freely spent what little money they had on clothing and entertainment. Constanze often went to the spas in Baden, to rest and recover from her many pregnancies. Wolfgang had a loyal bond with Constanze, who some criticized as a poor household manager. The pair moved often, usually because of their fluctuating finances.

Mozart could be personally frivolous, but he was never frivolous with or flippant about his music. He worked well under pressure, often completing pieces at the very last possible moment, working through many nights, with Constanze helping to keep him awake.

Mozart had a steady flow of students, providing a reliable if paltry income. At the Mozart home, most mornings were filled with lessons; afternoons with social lunches, meetings, and gatherings; and evenings with performances. Mozart was a master of improvisation, and thoroughly enjoyed playing music with his friends

Above: Frontispiece to the six quartets dedicated to Joseph Haydn. Below, left: The dedication page of the same series of quartets.

and colleagues. Joseph Haydn heard some of Mozart's quartets, and called him a "great" composer. Mozart would later dedicate six quartets to "Papa" Haydn, who always remained a close friend.

When he was not performing, Mozart worked almost continuously on new compositions. He began work on a major opera, *Le Nozze di Figaro* (The Marriage of Figaro), K. 492, in 1785.

Le Nozze di Figaro

*L*e Nozze di Figaro tells the story of Figaro, valet to the Count, and Susanna, maid to the Countess Almaviva. While Figaro and Susanna are discussing their marriage and which room they should live in afterward, Susanna tells Figaro that the Count has been hinting at meeting with her, and a room so close to his might be unwise. The Count may exercise his right to romance his servant before letting her marry. While Figaro is thinking about what to do, Dr. Bartolo and his maid Marcellina enter. Dr. Bartolo has a grudge against Figaro, and Marcellina wants to marry him. In fact, she once lent money to Figaro, and he made a promise to marry her if the money was not returned on time. She wants to cash in on the promise, causing Dr. Bartolo, who has designs on Marcellina, to dislike Figaro even more.

Once Susanna is alone again, a young page named Cherubino comes to tell her that he is in love with the Countess. He is, it seems, always in love with one woman or another. While they are talking, the Count comes to the room, so Cherubino hides, inadvertently hearing the Count proposition Susanna. The Count likewise hides when he hears Don Basilio, the music master, at Susanna's door. Don Basilio gossips about Cherubino's attentions to the Countess, causing the Count to reveal himself. Now the Count tells stories about Cherubino and the gardener's daughter, Barbarina (remember, Cherubino is fickle), and discovers Cherubino's presence in the room. Suddenly Figaro comes back in with a group of peasants, all praising the Count for letting Susanna marry, and the Count is coerced into behaving graciously, for the moment.

The Countess, saddened because the Count is quickly losing interest in her, contrives a plot with Susanna and Cherubino. They write a letter to the Count, supposedly from Susanna, agreeing to meet him later that night. The original plan is for Susanna and the Countess to switch clothes, but eventually, it is Cherubino who dresses as Susanna for the tryst. In the meantime, Dr. Bartolo, Don Basilio, and Marcellina tell the Count that he must instruct Figaro to marry Marcellina, not Susanna. In an effort to escape this predicament, Figaro protests he can't marry because his parentage is unknown, and in the ensuing conversation, he mentions a birthmark which reveals him to be the son of Marcellina and Dr. Bartolo. Of course, Susanna finds Marcellina and Figaro embracing as mother and son, but she thinks they're embracing as lovers.

There is a great deal of confusion for all the characters in the final act when both men are making love to the wrong woman. Figaro manages to decipher the ruse and even to have some fun with it, but by the end, the Count is forced to reveal himself as a great fool. He begs his wife's forgiveness, while Figaro and Susanna commence their life together.

*Illustration of Susanna, Figaro's
betrothed in* Le Nozze di Figaro.

Le Nozze di Figaro

Figaro was a controversial undertaking for Mozart. He did not yet have a reputation as a successful opera composer, and therefore he could not expect Emperor Joseph II to readily endorse the production. This was Mozart's first collaboration with the Italian poet Lorenzo da Ponte, whose talents were largely unknown. But the two men had a similar goal: to produce an opera that would appeal both to royalty and to general audiences.

Originally a play written by the Frenchman Pierre de Beaumarchais, *Figaro* had been banned as being too risqué. Among other complaints, it did not conform to the contemporary formula for opera buffa: it was too long and had too many characters. But da Ponte and Mozart convinced each other they could make a successful opera, and they worked on it discreetly to avoid censure.

As rumors about *Figaro* began to leak, first of its existence and then of its excellence, jealous competitors began conspiring to sabotage the production by condemning the opera as lewd. But da Ponte stayed one step ahead of his enemies, convincing Emperor Joseph II at the last minute that *Figaro* had been sufficiently "sanitized." He pledged that all offensive parts had been removed and that the finished work was a production of which the Emperor would be proud.

The opening performance was held on May 1, 1786. There are conflicting accounts of just how it was received. Not surprisingly, to many of the principals, *Figaro* was a magnificent success even before the first note was struck. It may be a measure of the opera's popular acceptance that after the first several performances, the number of encores the company would perform had to be limited.

Figaro was unconventional in several important respects, not the least significant of which was its portrayal of aristocrats as buffoons. To have servants mocking their royal masters onstage was certainly a change, and many thought an affront, to the status quo. But *Figaro* was also a musician's dream. Its entire story unfolded musically. Up until *Figaro*, opera music had had to acquiesce to the story, often resulting in "story-telling" breaks in the music. In *Figaro*, the music is the storyteller.

Eine Kleine Nachtmusik

A composition for strings entitled *Eine Kleine Nachtmusik* (A Little Night Music), K. 525, was also written in Vienna during the late 1780s. This cantata has become one of Mozart's most famous pieces, yet it is also one of his most puzzling. It does not resemble any of the other works he produced at the time; it is much more like his earlier work. In fact, he had also called an earlier piece *Nachtmusik*.

Vienna in 1787, the year Beethoven arrived to study with Mozart.

Prague (circa 1787), where Le Nozze di Figaro *was an enormous success.*

The two compositions have nothing in common except their title; perhaps "night music" was simply a descriptive term with a special meaning known only to Mozart. Whatever the motivation or inspiration, this quintet is one of Mozart's most famous and well-loved compositions.

Leopold's Death

In April of 1787, Wolfgang, recently returned from his triumphant visit to Prague, where *Le nozze di Figaro* had been a resounding success, learned that Leopold was very ill. At the beginning of the month, Wolfgang wrote a letter to his father in Salzburg that not only expressed his hopes for the elder Mozart's speedy recovery, but also revealed Wolfgang's familiar, even intimate, attitude toward death: "I need hardly tell you how greatly I am longing to receive some reassuring news from yourself. And I still expect it; although I have now made a habit of being prepared in all affairs of life for the worst. As death, when we come to consider it closely, is the true goal of our existence, I have formed during the last few years such close relations with this best and truest friend of mankind, that his image is not only no longer terrifying to me, but is indeed very soothing and consoling! And I thank God for graciously granting me the opportunity...of learning that death is the key which unlocks the door to our true happiness. I never lie down at night without reflecting that—young as I am—I may not live to see another day." On May 28, Leopold died, leaving Mozart bereaved, but not destroyed; he was no stranger to death, even at the age of thirty-one, having lost by this time his mother, two children, and numerous friends and colleagues.

Don Giovanni

Le Nozze di Figaro was a huge success in Prague. Mozart and Constanze were invited there during its run to enjoy the amenities of the city and the admiration of its citizens. While in Prague, Mozart was commissioned by a local impresario and theater company owner, Pasquale Bondini, to write the opera *Il Dissoluto punitio, ossia il Don Giovanni*, K. 527. Mozart returned to Vienna to enlist the services of da Ponte, and they began work on the new opera immediately.

Leporello, the servant in Don Giovanni.

True to form, Mozart completed the now-famous overture the night before the opera's premiere, and he copied it himself. *Don Giovanni* was a great success from

Freemasonry

Around 1783, Mozart became a freemason. Organized as the Grand Lodge of England in 1717, freemasonry was an organization designed to promote social and charitable togetherness between men of different social origins. Mozart joined a lodge in Vienna, although he also visited lodges in Germany and France. He composed music as a mason; *Die Maurerfreude*, K. 471, *Maurerische Trauermusik*, and the opera *Die Zauberflöte* (The Magic Flute), K. 620,

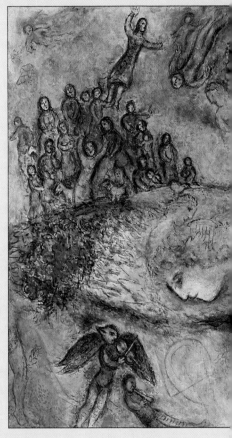

Marc Chagall's interpretation of Die Zauberflöte.

Example of a freemason initiation, where the candidate is symbolically buried, then reborn as a mason.

are specific examples. In 1785, both Joseph Haydn and Leopold Mozart, during the latter's last visit to his son, became freemasons. Voltaire and George Washington were also members. It is believed that in the late 1780s Mozart began to formulate the idea for a separate organization that would promote the idea of equality between men and women (freemasonry was strictly for men).

Josef Hoffman illustrations from the 1869 opera performance of Die Zauberflöte, *a fairy tale with underlying references to freemasonry.*

Karl Thomas Mozart, born in 1784.

the moment of its debut in Prague in October of 1787, but it was appreciated less in Vienna, where it opened in May of the following year. To some critics, *Don Giovanni*, which touches on the supernatural, was immoral. Many others believed it to be the greatest opera ever composed.

Despite Mozart's popularity and successes, there was again relatively little money coming in. As usual, when the Mozarts' income decreased, so did their fanciful lifestyle. Mozart accumulated debts and owed money to friends and patrons.

Salon of the Prague home where Mozart entertained friends in 1787.

In late 1787, Mozart was appointed *Kammermusicus* (chamber musician) to the emperor's court in Vienna, but with only a small salary. (Joseph II paid Mozart less than he had his predecessor, a situation that did not please the temperamental composer.) Constanze gave birth to her fourth child, their first girl, but she, too, died in infancy. The Mozarts had only one living son, Karl Thomas, who was born in 1784. In 1788, Mozart composed the Piano Concerto in D Major, K. 537, and what would become his last three symphonies, Nos. 39, K. 543, 40, K. 550, and 41 ("Jupiter"), K. 551.

Lorenzo da Ponte

Da Ponte was a poet with a colorful personality. He had been banned from Venice as an adulterer. In Vienna, his first appointments as a librettist had been with Mozart's greatest competitor, Antonio Salieri. These works weren't very successful, and this, coupled with his distrust of Salieri, made Mozart reluctant to work with da Ponte on *Le Nozze di Figaro*. Nevertheless, theirs turned out to be a very successful working relationship. Da Ponte used the controversial aspect of the opera to stir up public interest, then convinced Emperor Joseph II it would not be controversial. After the immediate success of *Le Nozze di Figaro*, the two men went on to collaborate on *Don Giovanni* and *Cosi fan tutte*.

Italian poet Lorenzo da Ponte collaborated with Mozart on three important operas.

Da Ponte also worked in London and New York, apparently stirring up scandal wherever he went. He died in 1838.

Mozart was fond of entertaining in small gatherings such as this.

Symphony No. 40 in G Minor and the Late Works

It is not possible that Mozart knew these were his final three symphonies, yet they are among his greatest works, especially Symphony No. 40 in G Minor, K. 550 (1788). There is no record that any of the symphonies were performed

Mozart's fortepiano, now at the Mozart Museum in Salzburg.

This 1789 silverpoint drawing of Mozart is by Doris Stock.

publicly while Mozart was alive, yet his attention to them is unquestioned, particularly as regards the No. 40 symphony, which is considered one of the most structurally, thematically, and harmonically perfect works ever composed. Mozart's life was in turmoil at this time, but his music remained unscathed.

Anonymous portrait of Mozart as Knight of the Golden Spur, 1777.

A Wealth of Correspondence

The richest source of information about Mozart's life and his family is the vast correspondence to, from, and about him. Leopold Mozart felt strongly that letters were an important way to preserve history; his letters often have a tone that suggests he expected them to be read by others. Some of the earliest correspondence begins with the Mozart family's first travels. Because he had borrowed money from his Salzburg landlord, Lorenz Hagenauer, Leopold wrote faithful accounts of their journeys, including details on how the money was spent. Whenever they were separated, letters were continuously written by family members to one another. When traveling only with Wolfgang, Leopold wrote frequent, detailed, even suggestive, letters to his wife, Anna Maria. At first, Wolfgang wrote postscripts to Leopold's letters, addressed to his mother and sister. Letters to Leopold, when Wolfgang was on his own, detail his efforts to find work, his opinions about people he met and the music he heard, and his interest in Constanze. Wolfgang also wrote to his sister and to his cousin Bäsle in Augsburg. After his father's death, most of Wolfgang's letters were to Constanze during their periods of separation, and they reflect the genuine love between the two. During his last travels to Dresden, Frankfurt, and Munich, Mozart also wrote to some of his students who had become good friends.

Part of letter from Anna Maria to Leopold Mozart as she traveled with Wolfgang.

Portion of a 1783 letter from Wolfgang, in Vienna, to Leopold.

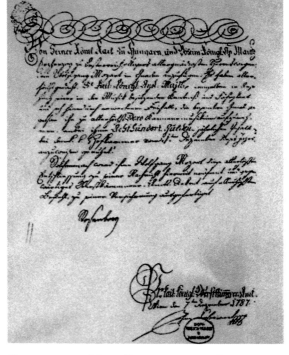

Decree appointing Mozart Kammermusicus *to the court, 1787.*

Mozart embarked on a concert tour to Berlin in 1789, making stops in Dresden, Leipzig, and Prague. In Berlin he played for the queen and king, who requested that he write six string quartets. Mozart was able to complete three of the quartets, but died before completing the remainder.

In late 1789, Emperor Joseph II commissioned Mozart to write an opera buffa, and he and Lorenzo da Ponte began work on *Cosi fan tutte*, K. 588. This comedy is about two men who decide to test the fidelity of their lovers by trying to seduce each other's partners. The opera opened on January 26, 1790, and closed in February, when Joseph II died.

The Piano Concerto in D became known as the "Coronation" because Mozart performed it during the enthronement period for the new emperor, Leopold II. But Leopold II had little appreciation for music, and less for Mozart. Aware of this, Mozart bravely swallowed his pride and wrote to Leopold II asking to be appointed assistant *Kappellmeister*, but the Emperor did not oblige. He further insulted Mozart by not inviting him to perform during a visit from the king of Naples.

Franz Xavier Wolfgang Mozart, born in 1791.

Mozart was incredibly prolific during his thirty-fifth, and last, year. He completed the festival opera *La clemenza di Tito* (The Mercy of Titus), K. 621, which was commissioned by the Bohemian Estates. He wrote the cantata *Die Maurerfreude* in honor of fellow masons around the world. He wrote the Clarinet Concerto in A Major, K. 622, and the hauntingly lovely *Ave verum corpus*, K. 618, for organ, strings, and voices. In September he conducted the opening of the opera *Die Zauberflöte*, commissioned in Vienna. This opera contained a heartfelt Masonic message of faith in humanism, and was a great success.

Mozart was seriously ill in the latter part of his thirty-fifth year. There has been great speculation about the circumstances surrounding and following Mozart's death. In his final months, he often thought he was being poisoned. This much is certain: in July of 1791, less than six months before he died, two events of significance occurred in Mozart's life — Constanze gave birth to their sixth child, Franz Xavier Wolfgang, and the Mozart home was visited by a mysterious messenger.

The day before his death, Mozart rehearsed the unfinished Requiem with friends.

Requiem in D Minor

The messenger was dressed in gray when he appeared at Mozart's door to commission the composition of a requiem mass. The commission had one provision: Mozart was not to ask or seek the identity of his patron.

The visitor was a representative of Count Walsegg, an amateur musician who wanted to honor his recently deceased wife with a requiem mass. Walsegg staged the mysterious charade because he planned to claim the piece as his own composition.

Antonio Salieri

Salieri was a conductor and composer at the same time as Mozart. In the mid-1770s he conducted Italian opera in Vienna; he was also composing operas at the same time the newcomer Mozart was composing his own. Mozart strongly believed that Salieri made several attempts to sabotage productions of *Le Nozze di Figaro* and *Cosi fan tutte*. It is certainly possible that Salieri felt his status as the emperor's favorite composer was threatened by Mozart's talents; it is also possible that he took steps to win commissions away from Mozart. Despite stories about the fierce competition between the two men, however, it is not likely that Salieri would engage in conduct that would jeopardize his own stature and reputation. During his final illness, Mozart said he felt that he had been poisoned, but there is no evidence he even suspected Salieri was behind it. Not long before Mozart died, he and Salieri became, if not friends, at least respectful peers. At Mozart's invitation, the older musician attended a production of *Die Zauberflöte* in 1791. Salieri later worked as a music instructor, teaching, among others, Beethoven, Schubert, and Liszt.

Antonio Salieri, one of Mozart's rivals.

Watercolor by E. Hutter of the Mozarts' house in Vienna, where Wolfgang died.

The commission might have gone unrecorded by history if, at the time, Mozart were not drifting in and out of his final, ultimately fatal, illness. Probably delirious, Mozart was occasionally convinced that the messenger had appeared to him from another world. He worked on it feverishly, literally on his deathbed, often believing it was his own requiem.

Constanze and her sister Sophie Haibel returned from the Baden spas in October to find Mozart ill but working hard. A student and copyist named Franz Xaver Süssmayr was helping complete the Requiem manuscript, at Mozart's direction. But by November 20, Mozart could no longer work. His hands and limbs were swollen and inflamed. He was completely exhausted. The two women tended to him and Süssmayr hovered nearby. On December 4, friends sang parts of the Requiem for him. Mozart sang an alto part, albeit with a weak voice. He died around 1 A.M. on December 5, 1791, two months before his thirty-sixth birthday; the Requiem in D Minor, K. 626, remained unfinished. The cause of his death was given as "heated miliary fever."

Even now, doctors continue to study, speculate, and try to identify a more specific cause of Mozart's death. Various interpretations of his symptoms have pointed in various directions. Kidney disease, rheumatic fever, and tuberculosis have all been suggested as possibilities. There is universal agreement on one

St. Stephen's Cathedral in Vienna, where Mozart was married in 1782 and eulogized in 1791.

thing: whatever the cause, Mozart's tragic death at so young an age prematurely deprived the world of an unparalleled musical genius.

Monument to Mozart in Vienna.

In life Mozart bequeathed a body of work to every musical form: operas, symphonies, chamber music, church music, concerti, dance music, and songs. Much of his work is still unsurpassed two hundred years after his death.

Stories are told that Mozart was completely destitute when he died and that his body was thrown into an unmarked pauper's grave, without ceremony and without even a marker to proclaim his final resting place. The truth is not quite so dismal. After a simple service at St. Stephen's Cathedral, Mozart

Handwritten list of Mozart's compositions from 1784.

was indeed buried in a common grave in the cemetery of St. Marx, a suburb of Vienna, but not because he was forsaken. Rather, in an attempt to save money, Emperor Joseph II had decreed the year before that the "frivolous" expense of funerals would be cut back. Mozart was a court retainer. His death happened to correspond with the implementation of the new court policy. His interment was somber and dignified. Later, a simple marker was placed near his grave.

Mozart did not finish the Requiem, but his wife arranged its completion, probably by Süssmayr. Having become aware of Count Walsegg's fraudulent intentions, Constanze decided to represent the finished piece as a complete work by her late husband. In a preemptive twist that surely would have pleased the boisterous Mozart, Constanze arranged a public production of the Mass, under her husband's name, before Walsegg could stage his own.

Constanze after Mozart

Many of Mozart's followers were impressed by the diligence with which Constanze organized Mozart's affairs after his death. Because he had been a salaried chamber musician at the time of his death, Constanze was able to extract a pension from the court. She arranged and sang in concerts of his works, sold some of his manuscripts, and managed his estate effectively, providing support for herself and her two sons. She met diplomat Georg Nikolaus Nissen in 1797; they married in 1809. Together, they collected and arranged material for *Biographie W. A. Mozarts Nach Originalbriefen.* Many of the letters between Mozart and Constanze were included in the text. Some of them, especially the more personal ones, were censored, presumably by Constanze or Nissen, who became well-known as a Mozart scholar. The *Biographie* was published in 1828 and remains an authoritative source of information.

Additional Listening

Concerto for Clarinet in A, K. 622

Concerto for Flute and Harp in C, K. 299

Concerto for Flute and Orchestra in G, K. 313

Concerto No. 15 for Piano in B-flat, K. 450

Piano Concerto No. 16 in D, K. 451

Piano Concerto No. 17 in G, K. 453

Piano Concerto No. 22 in E-flat, K. 482

Piano Concerto No. 24 in C Minor, K. 491

Piano Concerto No. 3 in G, K. 216

Violin Concerto No. 5 in A, K. 219

Don Giovanni, K. 527

Fantasia for Mechanical Organ in F Minor, K. 608

Six German Dances, K. 509

Horn Concerto No. 2 in E-flat, K. 417

Horn Concerto No. 4 in E-flat, K. 495

Mass in C Major ("Coronation"), K. 317

Six Minuets, K. 599

Le Nozze di Figaro, K. 492

Quartet for Piano and Strings in G Minor, K. 478

Quintet for Clarinet and Strings in A, K. 581

Quintet for Piano and Winds in E-flat, K. 452

Requiem in D Minor, K. 626

Rondo for Piano in A Minor, K. 511

Serenade in D Major for Orchestra ("Haffner"), K.250

Solemn Vespers of the Confessor, K. 339

Sonata for Fortepiano and Violin in C, K. 296

Sonata for Fortepiano and Violin in E-flat, K. 380

Sonata for Organ and Orchestra in C, K. 329

String Quartet in G, K. 387

String Quartet in C Major ("Dissonant"), K. 465

String Quintet in D, K. 593

String Quintet in E-flat, K. 614

Symphony No. 31 in D ("Paris"), K. 297

Symphony No. 35 in D ("Haffner"), K. 385

Symphony No. 36 in C ("Linz"), K. 425

Symphony No. 38 in D ("Prague"), K. 504

Symphony No. 40 in G Minor, K. 550

Symphony No. 41 in C ("Jupiter"), K. 551

Die Zauberflöte, K. 620

For Further Reading...

Anderson, Emily. *The Letters of Mozart and his Family.* London: Macmillan and Co., 1938.

Blom, Eric. *The Master Musicians Series: Mozart.* London: J. M. Dent and Sons, 1935.

Einstein, Alfred. *Mozart—His Characters, His Work.* London: Oxford University Press, 1945.

Landon, H. C. Robbins, and Donald Mitchell, eds. *The Mozart Companion.* New York: Oxford University Press, 1956.

Marshall, Robert L. *Mozart Speaks.* New York: Schirmer Books, 1991.

Photography and Illustration Credits

Art Resource, pp. 29, 33, 53, 56 bottom, 58 top; Giraudon/Art Resource, pp. 18 top, 21, 22, 32, 49; SCALA/Art Resource, pp. 44 top, 45 top, 46, 55 top, 59 bottom; Courtesy of the Bertarelli Archives, Milan, p. 64; Courtesy of the British Library, p. 67; Deutsche Staätsbibliothek Berlin, p. 60 bottom; FPG International, p. 10; Courtesy of the Mozart Museum, Salzburg, Austria, pp. 19, 36 bottom, 40, 42; New York Public Library, pp. 8, 14, 15 bottom, 16 top, 20 top, 23, 24, 25 both, 26, 30 bottom, 31 top, 34 bottom, 36 top, 37, 38 top, 39 bottom, 41, 43, 45 bottom, 47 top, 51, 52, 54 left, 55 bottom, 59 top; North Wind Picture Archives, pp. 11 top, 12, 16 bottom, 17 top, 20 bottom, 58 bottom, 66 top; Universitätsbibliothek Prague, p. 60 top.

Reprinted with permission from TFH Publications Inc., *Mozart: His Life and Times,* pp. 18 bottom, 30 top, 31 bottom, 34 top, 35 bottom, 38 bottom, 39 top, 56 top, 57, 61 top, 62, 63, 66 bottom.

Cover collage images: © Rudy Muller/Envision, © M.K. Rothman/FPG International, Giraudon/Art Resource, SCALA/Art Resource, © Amy Reichman/Envision.

Index

A

Abduction from the Seraglio, 41
Academia Filarmonica, 30
Artaria (music publisher), 42
Ascanio in Alba, 30
Augsburg, 17
Ave verum corpus, 62

B

Bach, Johann Christian, 12,
    22, *22*
Bach, Johann Sebastian, 12,
    13, 22
The Barber of Seville, 32
Baroque era, 12, 22
Beaumarchais, Pierre de, 32,
    50
Beethoven, Ludwig van, 64
*Biographie W. A. Mozarts
    Nach Originalbriefen*
    (Nissen/C. Mozart), 67
Bohemian Estates, 62
Bondini, Pasquale, 53
Brussels, 17
Bullinger, Father Joseph, 38

C

Catholicism, 11
Chagall, Marc, 55
Clarinet Concerto in A
    Major, 62
Clementi, Muzio, 43, *43*
Colloredo-Waldersee,
    Hieronymous von
    (Prince-Archbishop of
    Salzburg), 33, *34*, 40
Copyists, 27
Cosi fan tutte, 57, 61, 64

D

da Ponte, Lorenzo, 50, 53, 57,
    57, 61
Don Giovanni, 53, 56, 57

E

Eine Kleine Nachtmusik, 51-52
"Elvira Madigan," 44-45
*Die Entführung aus dem
    Serail*, 41

F

Ferdinand (Archduke, Holy
    Roman Empire), 34
Firmian, Count Karl Joseph,
    43
Florence, 28, *31*
Francis I (Habsburg emperor), 8
Freemasonry, 54, 62
French Revolution, 16

G

George III (King of England),
    20, *20*
Grand Lodge of England, 54

H

Haffner, Siegmund, 43
Hagenauer, Lorenz, 60
Haibel, Sophie, 65
Handel, George Frederick,
    12, *13*
Haydn, Franz Joseph, 12,
    13, 46 ,*47*
Haydn, Johann Michael,
    13, *13*
Hoffman, Josef, 55
Holy Roman Empire, 8, *15*, *24*

I

Idomeneo, 40
Italy, 27, 28-31

J

Joseph II (Emperor, Holy
  Roman Empire), *15*, 40,
  43, 50, 57, 61, 67

K

Kammermusicus, 61
Kappellmeister, 3, 9, 11, 61
Köchel, Ludwig Ritter von,
  19, *19*
Konzertmeister, 39

L

La finta giardiniera, *31*
La finta semplice, 27, 43
Leopold II (Emperor, Holy
  Roman Empire), 61
Liszt, Franz, 64
London, 17, *25*
Louis XV (King of France),
  17
Lucio Silla, 30

M

The Magic Flute, 54, *55*, 62,
  64
Mantua, 28
Maria Feodorovna (Grand
  Duchess of Russia), 43
Maria Thérèse (Empress,
  Holy Roman Empire),
  15, 16, *16*, 34
Marie Antoinette, (Queen of
  France), 16
Marriage of Figaro, 32, 47-51,
  52, 53, 57, 64
Mass in C Minor, 44
Die Maurerfreude, 54
Maurerische Trauermusik, 54
Maximilian Joseph III
  (Elector of Bavaria), 14

Mercy of Titus, 62
Milan, 28
Missa Brevis in D Minor, 39
Mitridate, ré di Ponto, 30, 31,
  43
Mozart, Anna Maria
  (mother), 23, *23*
  death, 37-38
Mozart, Constanze (wife),
  40, 41-42, *41*, 44, 46,
  47, 53, 57, 60, 63, 65,
  67
Mozart, Franz Xavier (son),
  44, 62, 63
Mozart, Karl Thomas (son),
  44, 56, 57
Mozart, Leopold (father),
  14, 15, 17, *21*, 23, *23*,
  24, 25, 27, 34, 39,
  41-42, 60
  death, 52-53
  illness, 20
Mozart, Nannerl (sister), 10,
  11, *16*, 20, *21*, 22, 25,
  26, 34, 38
Mozart, Wolfgang Amadeus,
  15, 16, *17*, *21*, 23, 25,
  29, 42, 58, 59, 63, 66
  birthplace, 10, *10*
  death, 65-67
  health, 23-25
  illness, final, 63-65
  as prodigy, 14-17, 20-22
Mozart Museum, 20, 58
Munich, 14, 17, 31
Music
  court, 8
  instrumental, 12
  opera, 12, 27, 30, 31, 32,
    40, 41, 47, 50
  religious, 8, 11, 12, 30

serenatas, 30
sonatas, 19
symphonies, 20

N
Naples, 28
Nissen, Georg Nikolaus, 67
Le Nozze di Figaro, 32, 47-
51, 52, 53, 57, 64

O
Opera, 12, 30, 31, 32, 40, 41,
47, 50
Order of the Golden Spur,
30, 59

P
Paris, 17, 19, 35, 37, 38, 39
Piano Concerto in D Major
("Coronation"), 57, 61
Piano Concerto in D Minor,
45
Piano Concerto No. 21 in C
("Elvira Madigan"), 44-45
Prague, 52, *52*, 53

R
Requiem in D Minor, 64-65,
67
Rome, *30*

S
Salieri, Antonio, 57, 64, *64*
Salzburg, 8, 15, 17, 28, 31,
34, 39, *39*, 40
Schrattenbach, Count
Sigismund von (Prince-
Archbishop of
Salzburg), 9, 11, 27
Schubert, Franz, 64
*Search for a Basic Violin
Method* (L. Mozart), 11

Serenade in D Major for
Orchestra ("Haffner"),
43
Sonata for Violin in A
Major, 38
Süssmayr, Franz Xaver, 65,
67
Swieten, Baron Gottfried
Bernhard van, 43
Symphony No. 1 in E-flat,
20, 22
Symphony No. 4 in D Major,
22
Symphony No. 36 in C
Major ("Linz"), 43
Symphony No. 40 in G
Minor, 58-59
Symphony No. 41 in C Major,
("Jupiter"), 57

T
Thekla, Maria Anna (Bäsle),
35, 36
Thun-Hohenstein, Count
Johann Joseph Anton,
43

V
Venice, 28, *28*
Verona, 28
Victoria (Queen of
England), 18
Vienna, 15, 17, 24, 26, 45,
51, 66

W
Weber, Aloisia, 35, *35*, 40
Weber, Constanze. *See*
Mozart, Constanze

Z
Die Zauberflöte, 54, 55, 62, 64